IMMIGRATION

IMMIGRATION

A STUDY IN ARROGANCE AND IGNORANCE

EVAN HEASLEY

authorHOUSE®

AuthorHouse™ UK Ltd.
1663 Liberty Drive
Bloomington, IN 47403 USA
www.authorhouse.co.uk
Phone: 0800.197.4150

Published by AuthorHouse 08/19/2013

ISBN: 978-1-4918-7571-1 (sc)
ISBN: 978-1-4918-7572-8 (e)

CONTENTS

IMMIGRATION – A STUDY IN ARROGANCE AND IGNORANCE

The issue of immigration has probably been one of the most divisive issues of our time. It has divided people's opinion and has become a political hot potato which no mainstream politician has really tackled, or wanted to tackle.

What I have found when talking about this issue is, that for many people they have either been too frightened to express their opinion (for fear of being labelled a racist), or have not truly understood the reality of immigration and this devastating policy. What I need to state clearly is that we do not have a problem with immigration, but we do have a problem with **'mass immigration.'**

So, when writing about this issue, I want to look at a number of different areas, and I want to explain why I feel mass immigration has been a disaster for this country. I want to destroy some myths and explore how this policy has brought many more problems than benefits. Throughout my writing I will use the word immigration instead of mass immigration, but I am talking about the latter. You will find all my sources listed at the end of this book.

I want to emphasize that the issue of immigration is a different one to that of genuine asylum seekers (those fleeing for their lives from persecution). Great Britain has always been a country which has accepted genuine asylum seekers, and long may it continue.

Up until about 1997, this country saw our population grow annually by between 30,000 and 50,000 due to net immigration **(1)** (you work out net immigration by subtracting those who emigrate and those who immigrate into the country, and this will give you the net immigration figure), and this was never a problem. And, to be honest, immigration was never an issue which people brought up in discussion, or politicians ever worried about. This all changed when New Labour was elected in 1997, and opened up the door.

When writing this, I wanted to try and steer away from party politics, but having watched as a policy of mass uncontrolled immigration has been forced upon the British people, it is very difficult to keep away from it.

The EU Treaty of Nice came into being on the 1 February 2003; this basically increased the size of the EU from 14 to 27 members. On top of this, in 2004, 'EU Directive 2004/38/EU on the free movement of labour' became law in all member states. The UK, along with Sweden and Ireland decided to allow all new countries which had joined the EU to have free movement of labour straight away. A clause was put in this directive which meant it did not have to be enforced until 1 May 2011. The reason for the clause was for countries to ready themselves for a mass influx of foreign labour. But our government chose to allow free movement straight away. This meant that anyone who lived within the EU could move to this country and work and there was nothing anyone could do about it. As you can imagine this has created many problems; many at the time told the government that their estimates of how many would come to this country were way under, but they chose to ignore it.

In 2004, the door was opened up to free movement from the poorer states of Eastern Europe. The Labour government stated that about 13,000 Eastern Europeans would come to the UK in 2004 and about the same the year after. As it was, they were a little bit out on their estimates: in 2004, about 600,000 came to this country and the following year saw about another 600,000 arrive on our shores. So in two years our population grew by about 1.2 million due to immigration from Eastern Europe alone. (2) The most recent census figures show that the percentage of our population born abroad has risen in ten years. In 2001, it was 4.3 million, in 2011 it had risen to 7.5 million, which is an increase of over 3 million (3). That figure will have changed even more in the past two years since the census, so the impact on our population cannot be exaggerated.

I have listened to many politicians justifying the uncontrolled policy of mass immigration by saying these people were coming to this country to do work that British people did not want to do: but is this strictly true? When looking at this issue of British workers not wanting to work, you also have to look at Labour's disastrous policy of handing billions of pounds in benefits to many people, in the vain hope that this would eradicate poverty in this country.

The idea of giving the poorest in our society money so they could have a better living and have more money in their pockets to spend on food and other essentials sounds very altruistic. But I also believe it was very naïve to do this, and has been shown not to have worked. We now have many households in this country who have no-one at work and many who have never worked, simply because there is no incentive.

Before Labour opened up the door to migrants most businesses employed just British workers, or very few foreigners. Before Gordon Brown decided to increase the welfare budget most people found they were better off if they worked. After he started handing out billions in benefits many found they were better off if they did not work, so they did not.

With immigration on such a massive scale, the wages of the lowest paid dropped dramatically as businesses found it was better and cheaper to employ a migrant worker than a British worker (especially those at the bottom of the economic scale, as the vast majority of those coming here have ended up being employed in low paid jobs). This meant that even if a British worker wanted to work it wasn't worth their while doing so, simply because they would lose too much money from benefits. A number of studies have looked into the issue of immigration and the impact upon post industrial countries like the UK. These studies have come to the conclusion that it has a negative impact upon the indigenous people of that country, driving down wages, thus not making it worth working.

IT'S ABOUT SPACE, NOT RACE

O ver the past nearly ten years we have watched as the amount of people coming to this country has continued to remain in the hundreds of thousands; at this rate of population growth it is expected to hit about 70 million by about 2029. **(4)** England is now the most densely populated country in Europe (it was Holland until 2010).

England is now the 3rd most densely populated country in the world after South Korea and Bangladesh (this is with countries of more than 10 million).

Russia (largest country in the world with 11 time zones): population about 143 million (January 2013). The UK has a population about 43% of Russia and you could fit the UK into Russia about 70 times.

Canada (2nd largest country): population about 35 million (2012).

Australia (6th largest country): population about 23million (2013).

Argentina (8th largest country): population 41 million (2010)

Kazakhstan (largest landlocked country): population 15.4 million (2012).

New Zealand (about 10,000 sq miles bigger than the UK): population about 4.4 million (2012).

Norway (about 25,000 sq miles bigger than the UK): population about 5 million (2013).

Sweden (about 64,000 sq miles bigger than the UK): population about 9.5 million (2012).

Thailand and France have similar size populations but are both over twice the size of the UK.

Last fact; the state of Wyoming in the USA is 3,000 sq miles bigger than the UK but has a population similar to the county of Suffolk (UK), about 600,000.

If you have travelled to any country in Europe, or around the world you will very quickly realise how crowded this country really is. I could list many more countries, but if you spend any time to research this issue, you will very quickly realise that the UK has a very large population in comparison to its landmass.

With an increase in population and very limited space this brings many problems. And, I do not believe these problems have been seriously looked at or taken into the equation. When you allow unlimited immigration you cannot ignore the consequences of that policy, and the impact it has, not just nationally but also locally as well.

INFRASTRUCTURE

Within most towns and cities, there has been a constant pressure on our already overburdened infrastructure. These include pressure on housing, schools, hospitals, health clinics, doctors surgeries, transport links (roads, rail), water supplies (that is, having enough water for the population, especially in the driest parts of the country, the South East and East), sewage (upgrading of the existing mains to cope with extra housing and population) and energy supplies.

Currently the government is looking to reform the planning process to make it easier for developers to build houses and industrial units. It could be argued that this is a good thing; with a growing population we need more houses, and that makes sense. But many of the houses that are to be built are going to be out of reach for a large proportion of the population. I know that many new housing developments include a certain percentage of 'social housing', but as the population grows the amount of 'social housing' will not keep pace with the needs of a growing population.

The growing population, of course, includes a large percentage of migrants; in April 2010–April 2011 net immigration into this country increased from 198,000 and April 2009–April 2010 to 239,000 **(5)**. These people need somewhere to live, and the majority of them invariably will live in social housing, simply because it is all they can afford. On top of this, all councils from 1 May 2011 are under an obligation to treat all 'EU citizens' the same as British citizens. This means that if you are on the council housing list and someone comes from an EU country that has more children than you, their need will be deemed more important, and they will go above you. It does not matter how long you have waited, they will get a house before you.

Some will argue that this is fair, but I cannot agree with this whatsoever. What I have found when looking at this issue is that the vast majority of migrants who come to this country to work end up doing unskilled labour. Even if skilled workers arrive here it does not necessarily mean they will end up doing skilled work; Home Office figures show that of 18,780 skilled migrants who arrived in the UK in 2009 only 1 in 4 found skilled work **(6)**. When we then look at how this affects the housing stock, it is quite obvious that the already dwindling lower priced houses are soon swallowed up, which in turn means less to go around.

Many people are not affected by this issue, and many who argue in favour of continued immigration will never be affected. These people, many earning a good wage, do not have to worry about finding a house because they can afford to buy where they want. The simple fact is that the vast majority of migrants end up living in the poorer parts of our towns and cities. If you walk around a private housing estate with many nice, large, detached and semi-detached houses and knock on their doors you would be unlikely to find any migrants living in them. For many, immigration has brought a multitude of pressures, and the issue of housing is one them.

What I have generally found is that many middle class and wealthier people are not affected by a number of our social ills, like high crime and anti-social behavior, simply because they can afford to live in the areas where this does not happen. Those at the bottom of the economic scale cannot afford to move, so they have to make do with what they are given and what is available. This means that our dwindling housing stock is not expanding fast enough and those who are the poorest cannot find a house, simply because there are none.

In the 1960's, comprehensive schools arrived on the scene, and many thought this would somehow bring equality to our education system. The main problem with a comprehensive education system is that it reduces the standards and then ends up giving our children a sub-standard education that in many cases is not fit for purpose. This experiment has continued to this day; add to this the destruction of the grammar school system, and it does not take long to see that this experiment has not worked.

Those on the left (and many on the right) have sat, and not only watched but encouraged this destruction, and have never really considered the damage this has done to our children's education. Many of those who argue in favour of a comprehensive education invariable are in the fortunate position to live in an area which has good schools, or are wealthy enough to send their children to private schools. Those at the bottom do not have a choice but to send their children to the local comprehensive, and because there are no grammar schools there is no way many of those more able will achieve their full potential. My own experience of comprehensive education highlights something of what I am saying. My parents were not wealthy and had no choice but to send me to the nearest comprehensive school. The school I attended did not have a great reputation. The opportunity to take O' levels in certain subjects just was not there. I was amongst the last year to take exams under the old CSE and O' level curriculum, before the advent of GCSE exams. For those who never sat the old system, O' level exams were a higher standard than CSE, a grade one CSE was the equivalent of a grade C O' level. My strengths have always been the more literary subjects, in particular humanities subjects like history and religious studies. When it came to choosing what subjects I was to study to exam level I chose these two subjects along with the usual English, maths, etc. Unfortunately for me the school I attended did not run history and religious studies O' level courses so I was only able to do the CSE exam, and the highest mark I could achieve was a grade one CSE, and this I did. To be honest (and I do not want to sound too big headed) I achieved this without very little effort and no revision. I honestly believe I would have achieved a grade A O' level given the chance, this is an example from my own experience but I am sure if I spoke to many this would not have been an isolated example.

I have spent time looking at the background of some of our politicians, and one of the things I have realised is the complete hypocrisy of many of them. I won't name names, but if you look at some of the most high profile amongst their ranks you will see that they are often the worst offenders. Many do not send their children to the local school; they will send their children to a public school or at least to the very best state schools. This highlights how many of those in power, and who have wealth, do not truly understand the reality for so much of the population.

Again, if we look at our hospitals and doctors surgeries, the same applies. The government has stated it is going to continue to increase spending on the NHS, but the simple truth is, the amount being spent just cannot keep pace with the increase in population. This truth is simply being ignored; the creators of the NHS could not have foreseen how our society has changed, and the idea of a free health system for everyone in this country sounds fantastic, but can we really, as a country afford this luxury? As I am sure you are aware drug prices continue to increase, and so do many other things within the NHS, these include; wages, heating, food, medical equipment, hygiene goods, etc. With both a growing and an ageing population, this means that this already overstretched organisation is going to continue to buckle under the pressure. Put into the mix immigration, and you can only imagine what this is doing to the purse strings of the NHS.

In many maternity wards, some midwives are dealing with as many as four women who are in labour. This means that these women are not getting quality care, but also means that there is a greater chance of medical problems, sometimes complications which lead to fatal consequences. It does not help that we have a growing population, and, as all migrants are allowed the same treatment as British citizens, this puts extra pressure on our already overstretched maternity wards. I am sure if we look at most migrants you would find that the vast majority are of child bearing age or under. With many more people entering this country every week and entitled to the same care as any British citizen, it isn't any wonder they keep arriving. Who can blame them?

If you have travelled in most areas of the UK, particularly England, you will very quickly realise that our roads are under increasing pressure. With over 30 million vehicles on our roads it becomes very apparent that our road infrastructure is barely coping, and in many cases not coping at all. Every year our roads are patched up and more roads are built, but it only relieves the pressure for a short period. In the 1960's, Doctor Beeching cut many of our rail lines and stations, thus creating greater pressure on our roads, and as the years go by we can only watch as this pressure increases.

In the 1980's, the Conservatives under Margaret Thatcher went on a road building frenzy, and one of the outcomes of this was the dreaded M25. If you have travelled on this road at any time you will quickly realise that it isn't coping, and neither are many of our roads. This is not going to get any better; as our population continues to increase the amount of money being spent on them will decrease because of government cuts.

Our rail network has always been a bit of a joke, but what we are seeing is an increase in prices which means increasing pressure on people's finances. The government has agreed in principle to build a high speed rail link from London to Birmingham. They say this will reduce the travel time between London and Birmingham by about 30 minutes; the government has stated it is initially going to cost over £17 billion **(7)**. It has also announced plans to extend this further to Manchester and Leeds, with the price rising to an estimated £33 billion (HS2) **(8)**. A couple of reports recently have been published which have looked into the cost of HS2 and they have stated that this vanity project is going to cost more than £33 billion. Before a single piece of rail has been laid it is accepted that the £33 billion price tag is a woeful underestimate, which should be sounding alarm bells, even amongst our ostrich like politicians. Many people who have looked into the benefits (particularly the Taxpayers alliance) have stated there will be very little, because the cost of this rail link will have to be paid back. This will mean prices will be very high, and the likelihood is that only those with a good income will be able to travel on it.

Rather than spending £33billion on a rail link that is only going to make a limited difference in time between two or more cities, would it not be better to spend that money on the existing railway and bring back some of the old branch lines? This I believe would benefit everyone in the long run as it would mean less cars on the road, so less pollution, and the government could use some of that £33 billion to reduce the cost of travel to make it worthwhile, while making it more affordable to travel by rail.

Another benefit would be to take freight of the roads, which would then have a knock-on effect with less damage to our roads from large vehicles, so less spent on road works. There would be less time lost on traffic jams and delays, more companies would invest in this country because there would be many more places with rail links. The all round benefits to increased rail travel and cheaper rail travel would mean quality of life would be greater for many people. But I feel the government would not do this, which means more travel misery for the rest of us as our population grows.

Over the past few years, as our population has grown, more houses have been built; this has meant that these houses have had to be connected to the existing sewer network, and many of the sewer pipes were never designed to withstand the amount of sewage flowing through them. Unless the investment is put into this area we will see many problems increase. If the water companies are going to improve our sewer and water networks it is going to mean investment and this means greater costs to the consumer. Already people are struggling under an increase in prices, all of which just adds to the pressure.

This brings me onto energy. With more people we need more energy, that's obvious. The government has decided to follow a course of action which will ultimately bring this country to a halt or bring massive financial hardship to all of us. The people who are going to suffer the most, of course, are the poorest in society, particularly the elderly.

The government has decided to invest in 'green energy'. They are going to spend over £100 billion from 2010 to 2020 on building wind turbines **(9)**. The government is abiding by EU targets for renewable energy and has decided that wind is the best way forward. Which of course raises the major problem that the wind does not blow all the time, so you cannot rely on this form of energy, which will mean that we need some sort of back up. The government has plans to shut nine coal fired power stations by 2015, this will mean a total loss of 11.8 gigawatts of energy. What no-one is saying, is that the reason for this completely bonkers policy, which is the EU Industrial Emissions Directive 2010/75/EU. It defies any sort of logic, because when the wind does not blow we will have to import energy at massive expense. With a growing population, this is going to mean increasing pressure on our energy network and, of course, increased prices.

The government does not seem to be listening to reason on this whole issue and has decided to follow a very dangerous policy regardless of the consequences.

With the advent of Shale gas, and the potential for cheap energy, it makes sense if the government follow a sensible route and invests heavily in this amazing cheap energy source. Let's hope the government takes a sensible approach and decides to see reason in regards to their energy policy. But I am not holding my breath.

I have highlighted a few issues about our infrastructure and only looked at them very briefly, if the government does not take seriously these issues I have mentioned, we are heading for hard times. If you put into the mix continued mass immigration, you can only imagine that this will make matters even worse.

COUNCILS AND
THE PUBLIC SECTOR

Over the coming years, all local authorities and public sector bodies are going to have to make massive cuts. This will mean two things. Firstly, the ever smaller amount of money these bodies will be getting is going to have to go further, and secondly it will mean job losses.

As a population grows, the money that needs to be spent by local authorities will increase, this is logical; more rubbish collection, more school places needed, more social problems, etc. There are many more things I could name, but I am sure you get the general idea.

You could argue that migrants are working and paying taxes, so they then pay their way. This might possibly be true if they weren't using any of our country's services and just paying tax, but because many migrants settle with their families this does not work out in our favour. A large percentage of those coming to this country are employed doing jobs which pay the minimum wage. This means that their wage simply does not cover the cost of what they receive in terms of welfare, education for their children, the NHS and other services. Many studies have looked into this and I will quote from them later.

The government is cutting back on spending as a consequence of which the money local councils have to spend will be less, but will have to go further. Already many areas of the public sector are feeling the effect. Inevitably, it is those at the bottom of the socio-economic scale who are impacted the most. Many day care centres for the elderly and vulnerable adults are starting to close down; in my town it has already happened. Many areas are going to be affected, and as I have said it will mean those at the bottom of the economic scale who will feel the most pain.

Then we come to job losses. Over the next few years, it is expected that all public sector bodies are going to lay off workers **(10)**. Even services which you might think are essential for society to function will be affected, like the fire service and the police. Suffolk Fire and Rescue service has plans to reduce it's full time fire fighting establishment from 241 to 209 over the next 3 years, which is just one small example of what is happening, and continues to happen. With net immigration continuing to increase, and no chance that we are going to see a reduction, this will mean more and more people looking for less and less jobs.

The government has shown that jobs are being created in the economy. In May 2010, figures show that unemployment was running at 2.51 million **(11)**. The figures for the 3 months up until the end of March 2013 show that this figure has risen by 10,000 to 2.52 million **(12)**. Yet in that same time, the amount of jobs that have been created has increased immensely. Figures form the ONS **(13)** show that 499,000 jobs were created between October 2011 and October 2012 alone, but, as I have pointed out, the unemployment rate has not really fallen. Why is this?

We cannot ignore the elephant in the room, and that is immigration. Surely if, according to the government, (which states that over 1 ¼ million jobs have been created since May 2010) jobs are being created, this should mean that unemployment has in fact fallen. Even taking into consideration those losing jobs in the public sector we should have seen a drop in the unemployment rate. The simple fact is, that because we have uncontrolled immigration (it doesn't matter what the government says, they cannot control the influx of foreigners), it does not matter how many jobs are created, unemployment is not going to change that much. This is because the tide of immigration is going to continue and many employers have made it quite clear they would rather employ a foreign worker, so British workers (regardless of whether they are hard working and reliable) are always going to stand less of a chance than a foreigner.

It doesn't matter what the government does, they cannot control immigration, so unfortunately nothing is going to change. It does not matter how many jobs they create or are created, the simple fact is the majority will go to foreigners.

If you think that is an exaggeration, it isn't; the facts speak for themselves. In the 13 years that Labour was in power, 98.5 per cent of all jobs went to migrants. ONS figures show that in 1997 there were 1.64 million foreign born workers, which by the end of 2009 that had increased by 1.9 million to 3.5 million. The figures show that there were only an extra 25,000 extra British born workers in employment at the end of 2009 than there were when Labour came to power. Add into the mix 1.5 million public sector workers looking for work, you can only imagine the consequences of continued uncontrolled immigration **(14)**.

SOCIO-ECONOMIC IMPACT

In 2010, two local councillors from Peterborough, Keith Sharp and Charles Swift, wrote a letter to the three main party leaders explaining their concerns about immigration. This is what they said:

'At our local primary school, Fulbridge, which has a roll of 675 pupils, 27 different languages are spoken with only 200 of the pupils having English as a first language.

The first-year reception class has 90 pupils, of which only 17 are white British. Every day new arrivals are turned away. Registration at the local doctor's surgery has rocketed with more than 90 per cent of the new arrivals being from the EU. There has been a substantial increase in women who are pregnant. The Health Service and Primary Care Trust in the city have overspent by millions in the past year.'

A key issue is the Government's failure to support councils. And Mr Swift and Mr Sharp make clear that the local authority cannot track all new arrivals—crucial information in assessing what they need.

They say, 'there were only four EU citizens on the local electoral roll in 2004. Now there are 537 and we know there are substantially more here'.

The councillors also voiced the fear that immigration is fuelling a rise in crime.

'We had four police houses in the ward years ago. Everyone knew and respected the local constable. Now we have muggings, robberies, burglaries and neighbour disputes. We have prostitutes, drug dealers and an ever-increasing number of people who drive without road tax or insurance.'

The issue of rising crime and immigration is something that no politician wants to mention, for fear of being branded a racist. I know there are many indigenous people who are committing crimes, and I know there are many migrants who come to this country to work and do not commit any crimes. But the impact of immigration and crime needs to be looked at.

One of the reasons we need to look at the issue of crime and the impact of an increase caused by immigration is because all crime seems to be rising within the indigenous population; we don't want to add to these figures with those who shouldn't be in the country.

Crime is something that impacts upon many people, and there has been a massive increase in crime from those arriving from Eastern Europe. A survey of 8 police forces in 2008 found that there had been a 300 per cent increase in crimes committed by migrants from Eastern Europe over the previous three years **(15)**. This figure does not include those who come from outside the EU. As you can imagine, with our already overcrowded prisons and the increasing pressure the police and courts are under, this just does not help.

One fact which comes from the Metropolitan Police, is that in the first three months of 2011, detectives from the Dedicated Cheque and Plastic Crime unit identified 120 Romanians linked to ATM crime. DCI Paul Barnard of The Met said:

"The fact is 92 percent of all ATM fraud we see in this country is committed by Romanian nationals. Very, very tight communities, very tight gangs. The crime is highly lucrative earning the gangs well over £2 million a month and the competition is fierce." **(16)** This should concern everyone, because from 1 January 2014 our borders will be opened to the whole of Romania!

If you put into the mix the European Human rights Act, and the difficulty in expelling migrants from the country, it becomes increasingly clear that immigration is causing greater and greater problems.

These local councillors went on to write about the impact on housing and other areas:

'Some 16,000 migrants, many seeking farm work, have moved to the Peterborough area since 2004. Immigrant communities account for 64 per cent of the population growth. The arrival of so many migrants has left Peterborough's housing system in chaos, with immigrants sleeping rough and relying on the Salvation Army for food.

They say many properties have been bought by speculators and turned into multi-occupancy dwellings let to immigrants.

The consequence is that our housing waiting lists have rocketed and our homeless hostels are full. This reinforces reports of migrants living in makeshift huts along the local river and slaughtering swans to eat.

Mr Swift, 79, a former train driver and trade unionist who was awarded the OBE for his council services, said 'The political leaders must listen to ordinary people.

There must be a control on migrant numbers coming in. It is what people want.'

I do not think anything these councillors are saying is unreasonable, and these words are echoed across the country by many people, but the politicians are not listening.

Many people (usually politicians and those on the left) argue that immigration has broadened and enriched our society. They state that those coming to this country bring a richness to it, that we now live in a multi-cultural society, and that this can only be a good thing. Too many people who state this have never looked at the reality of this ill-thought out policy.

Many of those who speak about the benefits are not affected by the problems immigration brings, with jobs and houses becoming scarcer. Overcrowded schools, the impact of crime, money being scarcer within councils and having to go further, it is always the most vulnerable within our society which are affected the most.

I have always wondered why so many think that a multi-cultural society is such a great thing. It is like these people are saying a homogeneous, mono-cultural society is inherently bad, and a society which has many different cultures living within it is inherently good. Does this mean that countries which are dominated by one culture are less enlightened or somehow more closed and less open and tolerant, and less open to change? Does this mean that a tribe in the Amazon or Africa is inherently bad because they have one culture? I always find it strange that those who argue in favour of multiculturalism would also argue in favour of letting these tribes maintain their culture.

I just wanted to say something in regards to multiculturalism. To many people the idea of a multicultural society is so important, it is as if those who totally believe in it see it as the pinnacle of our evolutionary development. A society which can call itself truly multicultural is seen as a paradise, a utopia in which all peoples, races, cultures, religions, ideologies (as long as those ideologies agree with the prevailing, political correct point of view) are seen as equal, and should be treated as such. This last statement shows that the idea behind multiculturalism just cannot work.

For those who are believers, the idea that anyone could disagree with multiculturalism is tantamount to being in league with the most heinous of societies; they would be talked about as if they were the same as those who believe in a 'master race', like the Nazis and should be spoken of in those terms. This has become more apparent and this attitude has been enforced more and more. The recent case of two foster parents having the children under their care removed for being members of the United Kingdom Independence Party (which does not agree with multiculturalism) **(17)** highlights how far we have come. The prevailing ideology has now started to be seen as 'right' and any other point of view or belief is seen as 'wrong', and cannot be questioned. This ironically is how the Nazi leadership viewed their policy of a 'master race' during the 1930's and 1940's.

The idea behind multiculturalism is quite simple, but in itself it raises many questions, not least the paradox that those who push forward the belief in everyone being treated equally do not themselves believe that every opinion is equally valid. Surely, if you believe in a society that is one great melting pot of cultures, beliefs and religions, this should also mean that you accept everyone's beliefs? This, of course, cannot happen because so much of what many other cultures, religions and societies believe is counter to what those who believe in the religion of multiculturalism adhere to.

If you are a believer, and you believe that my beliefs and culture should be respected, surely that should be so. If you believe that any given culture is equal to another that should be so, no argument! But of course, this cannot happen. Those who are believers will state that all men and women should be treated the same regardless of sexual orientation or gender, and rightly so. But how does this weigh up with a society that treats women as second class citizens, that believes in forced marriages, and which not only views women as lesser human beings but, in which such attitudes are actually ingrained and part of the culture (as in many Muslim communities)? How does the belief in treating all people the same regardless of their sexual orientation stand up to scrutiny when there are societies which treat homosexuals as criminals, persecuting them and imprisoning them for being homosexual?

This is the paradox within the multicultural movement, 'I believe all men and women are the same, I believe all cultures are equal and should be treated as so, but I can only do that if they believe what I believe'. This goes against a truly multicultural belief system and shows how this belief has no solid foundation. The belief that all are the same cannot be true because, quite simply, those who have a different opinion or belief to the prevailing ideology are not seen or treated as the same or equal. Which in the end reveals this religion (for that is what it is) as having no logic or no true tenets. If we take the belief that all cultures, religions, ideologies, etc, should be treated the same, surely they should be treated as such, but they simply cannot under this belief system, for the reasons I have stated above. So, logic would dictate that a belief in a multicultural society is a belief in an unequal and ultimately dangerous society, stifling free speech, freedom of expression, freedom of religion, freedom of belief, eventually becoming an intolerant society that forces through laws to make any other opposing ideology illegal. This is the paradox of multiculturalism.

Now back to immigration. I am not saying that immigration does not bring benefits; I am not saying that it does not open up people's minds and attitudes, but what concerns me is that we are almost seeing the destruction of one culture in favour of the creation of another. Great Britain has changed, but that does not mean that change is always good or beneficial. Many within this country are sitting and watching as their towns and cities are changing before their eyes, and feel totally disconnected. Many of those people feel that they have no voice, and in some ways they do not. They look to their politicians for support, they look to them for representation, but when they speak out about this issue and their concerns, they are shouted down, they feel disenfranchised.

On a recent episode of BBC's Question Time (which was filmed in Boston, Lincolnshire), one question was asked about the potential for an influx of Bulgarian and Romanian immigrants in January 2014, and whether or not Britain's public services could cope, Cambridge University academic, Dr Mary Beard, who was on the panel, made reference to a report published by Boston Borough Council, saying: 'The most impressive single document I've read on this issue comes from Boston council and it's the task and finishing group report about the population change in Lincolnshire.' She continued:

'It answers the question about public services and looks very carefully about the changes in Boston over the last ten years. It does identify particular management issues with an influx of any kind of population, but what it makes absolutely clear is that we can cope with this and benefit from it. It's very clear, for example, that European migrants have a low use of the benefits system, a low use of the health care system and they take very, very small amounts of social housing. Only one per cent of social housing is actually occupied by people who are economic migrants. Public services can cope.'

But a local woman, Rachel Bull counter-argued and said that Boston's own high street was becoming like a "foreign country".

She said:

"I have a family that lives in Boston and we have land at Boston. We've had major issues with workers, they've nowhere to go and are camping on our land. We can't move them off because the police aren't interested. Boston, its surgeries and hospitals are at breaking point because of these people coming into the country and nothing is being done. There are hardly any locals here anymore because they're all moving away. It's got to stop."

This highlights the reality of the situation and how so many people actually feel that their country has changed and has become like a foreign country. This has been forced on the people of this country with no consent and with no consultation—basically no-one was asked whether they wanted it or not. Dr Beard then went on to make a joke about the local maternity hospital remaining open due to new births from migrants. The reaction of Dr Mary Beard and so many of her ilk highlights how totally out of touch they are!

Many people feel that this change has been forced upon them without ever being consulted, and do not think they are being listened to. Every poll that is taken shows that the issue of immigration is amongst the majority of people's top concerns. But what we have seen is politicians ignoring this issue. David Cameron has stated that he is going to reduce the amount of immigrants coming to this country from hundreds of thousands down to the tens of thousands, but the simple fact is this is not happening and is unlikely to change. In a recent report by the Public Administration Committee, it stated that "official migration figures for the UK are little better than a best guess". In the year to June 2012, immigration was estimated at 515,000 while emigration was estimated at 352,000, putting net migration at 163,000 **(1a)**. This makes a mockery of any promise David Cameron has made to reduce net immigration, they are simply not taking this issue seriously or are either unwilling or unable to do anything about it, I fear it is both!

I believe if this issue is not tackled, and tackled head on, we will start to see unrest and even violence between different racial groups. This sounds rather depressing, but I can see it happening; I have spoken to many people and without prompting, the issue of immigration comes up in conversation. We are not talking about jack-booted fascists, but normal ordinary people who are concerned about the change that has happened.

The letter from the Peterborough councillors was written at the beginning of 2010; it was not racially motivated and was well thought out and articulately written. You would think that an issue which concerns so many people would have elicited a sympathetic response. It did not! Not one of the main party leaders bothered to respond. I think this sums up the attitude of those in charge.

Many have argued that immigration has been beneficial because those who come to this country are doing the work which the majority of British people do not want to do. But what is the truth behind this statement? You would think when you hear this that British people are generally a lazy and snobbish people. "That work is below me, I wouldn't do that work even if you paid me £30,000 a year". These are things you might expect many British people to be saying if you believed everything that businesses and politicians are saying. It does not help British workers get work if our politicians are continually stating that British workers are useless. What chance do they stand of getting work?

But I believe the issue is more complicated and sadder than the simple statement, 'British people do not want to work.' There are about 2.5 million people unemployed in this country and, without a doubt, there are many who would not work even if you gave them a well paid job. But there are many who would love to work, but simply cannot because of the simple fact that there are not enough jobs. What I have found when researching this issue is that many who make the statement that 'Britain needs migrants,' and 'immigration is good for our economy' have never struggled to find a job, and are unlikely to lose their job because their job is not under threat from immigration. A politician does not need to worry about a foreigner getting his position because it isn't going to happen. Likewise, those in professional jobs have nothing to fear from immigration or a reduction in wages, because the vast majority of those coming to this country are unskilled.

Those who are coming to this country might be better educated and worthy of their jobs, and I won't argue that they are not. But this does not help get British people back to work. What is the point of creating jobs if companies are unwilling to hire British people? This means that the unemployment figures will never be reduced significantly because we will continue to see more migrants coming to the UK to find work.

Recently David Cameron visited India and stated he would like more students to come to the UK. He said:

"The fact is today, as we stand, and this is going to be the case going forward—there is no limit on the number of students who can come from India to study at British universities, no limit at all. And what's more, after you have left a British university, if you can get a graduate-level job there is no limit to the amount of people who can stay and work or the time that they can stay at work."

It could be argued that this makes sense; giving motivated, intelligent young people an opportunity to come to this country brings great benefits, which sounds very reasonable. In a globalized world, surely it makes good economic sense to encourage the right sort of migrant to come to this country so they can then help our economy? Quite simple really. Or is it?

On the face of it, it is; two points, however, need to be made. Firstly, the vast amount of migrants coming to this country are not skilled, and as my previous statistic has shown, 'of 18,780 skilled migrants who arrived in the UK in 2009, only 1 in 4 found skilled work' (18). There is no guarantee that there will be the skilled jobs for graduates when they leave university. This might be a long term aim, but that does not solve the issue of those who are unemployed today. What I find so strange about David Cameron's statement is that at no point has he ever talked about British young people and young British graduates? Does he believe that Indian and other foreign young people are actually better than our own young people? Maybe they are, but that is besides the point! If you are going to encourage young people to go on to university, surely it makes sense to ensure that there are the jobs for them when they leave? I know many of those going to university are taking what could be termed 'easy degrees', and when they leave there are not the jobs for them because they do not have the right qualification? That, however, is not the fault of the young person. If we are going to get our young people working (and as I write this, the most recent figure for September-November 2012 show that unemployment among those aged between 16 and 24 has risen), does it not make sense to bring to a halt this open door policy? I do not in any way think that unreasonable! There are those who will argue that we need the right type of migrant, who will bring the right sort of skills, which, in principle, I am not against. If we want young people to go to university so they can help our economy grow, why doesn't the government encourage pupils to take the right subjects at school so they can then study those subjects at university? This means we do not have to open up our doors to a vast mass of foreign students. Again, I do not think this unreasonable. In saying what he has said in India, I believe David Cameron has shown a lack of compassion, and does not truly understand the reality of life for so many people in this country. As Prime Minister of The United

Kingdom he has been elected by us, the British electorate, and by that simple fact, it is his duty to serve us and not a foreign master, and put the interest of us and not them first. Regarding this, I would like to make one more point. That is, that I am sure the majority of those coming here on the back of this policy will be genuine students, but I am also sure that some will not be. How do you police this and ensure that the latter do not slip through?

This country is in a recession and things are not likely to improve greatly in the near future, the government is making cuts in the public sector, this will mean more people out of work. Does it make any sense to continue to allow foreign workers and to encourage many more to flood the market when there are not enough jobs for those in this country already?

In February 2013, Costa Coffee announced it was opening a branch in Nottingham and advertised for eight jobs, it had 1700 applications, including graduates and managers **(19)**. These were not highly skilled or highly paid jobs, yet the amount of applications shows what the reality is for so many people. One young man about 19 years old (who was one of the lucky ones to get a job), said "I have been looking for a job for over two years", he continued "you begin to wonder what is wrong with you. I am so happy I can do normal things again rather than just scraping by". He wasn't working as a manager in this restaurant, he was washing dishes. How could it be argued that continued immigration from a vast pool of unskilled labour is somehow beneficial or morally right? There are quite clearly many indigenous people in this country who would love a job and are desperate for work. I do not understand how anyone can argue in favour of a policy which brings so much hardship to so many people?

I believe those who argue in favour of continued immigration and the benefits to our economy, do not truly understand the reality. Or maybe they do understand but are unwilling to do anything about it for some ideological reason, or because it brings them some benefit (personal or financial). I have already stated that business likes immigration because it brings cheap labour. For example, a friend of mine has two friends who are builders that have worked for a business man for a number of years. They are reliable and hard working, they have never caused him any problems and there have never been any complaints about their work. Recently, these two men were told that their services were no longer required. The reason was that this man decided to take on four Polish builders for the same price as the two English builders. You might argue that this is an isolated case, but it is not.

One other point in regards to migrant workers is the fact that most are coming from countries which are poorer than ours. The impact of mass immigration on our existing workforce is massive in terms of wages because the standard of living for so many of those who are coming to Britain is lower than ours. Because the vast majority of those who come to this country end up working in jobs at the lower end of the social scale the wages of those already working in jobs (such as caring, for example) are kept very low. It means they continue to work for the minimum wage, and never rise above that level, simply because there are so many migrant workers willing to fill their place. A friend of mine works as a carer and has done for many years, she recently applied for a job in a care home, she was the only English speaker to be interviewed. The job paid the minimum wage, she was expected to work nights for the same wage and would not receive any sick pay. Suffice to say, because she was unwilling to work for such a low wage at night she did not get the job.

In 2003, a study by the Dutch government said:

GDP will increase, but the increase will largely accrue to the migrants in the form of wages. The overall net gain in income to residents is likely to be small and might even be negative.

A report by the House of Lords select committee on economic affairs published in 2008, said:

[. . .] no systematic empirical evidence suggests that net immigration creates significant dynamic benefits for the UK resident population.

Uncontrolled, unrestricted open door immigration into the UK has meant that wages have been driven down and living costs have been driven up because of extra demand. On housing, the people at the bottom of the economic scale experienced this directly. By contrast, massive immigration of cheap labour may benefit an expanding and developing economy in a country with vast reserves of natural untapped resources, such as America in the 19th century.

Those who argue in favour of continued immigration usually do not understand or feel the impact. Those who are middle class or very wealthy do not feel it because, as I have said, their job is not usually impacted by migrants, as the vast majority of migrants are doing unskilled work. The middle class and wealthier do not feel the impact upon housing, because the vast majority of migrants live in the poorer areas of our towns and cities.

It is very easy to sneer at someone when they complain about something; likewise, it is very easy to moan when someone complains about the issue of immigration, especially when it does not impact on them. For many, this issue is a very important one; it impacts upon them and their community; it also means they do not stand a chance of getting a job because there aren't any, and the businesses that are taking on workers would rather employ cheap foreign labour. Many businesses will not take on British workers simply because they believe the foreign worker is better (and of course cheaper); and even if the British worker is just as good, they will not take the chance.

The job of the government is to protect the rights of its own people, which of course does not mean that those who come to this country should be abused or taken advantage of. The government should protect the interests of their own citizens first. They then can help other countries to develop their own economies by adopting sensible international trade policies.

WHAT IS THE ANSWER?

This is what I believe needs to be done.

First. We need to leave the EU; if we do not, there is nothing we can do about controlling immigration. Regardless of what the government says, there is nothing we can do about a large proportion of the immigration into this country. It is incredibly difficult to deport dangerous criminals because of the European Human Rights Act, as many high profile cases have proven. A recent case highlights the ridiculous situation we have arrived at in this country. A Polish migrant Mariusz Krezolek was convicted of torturing and murdering his stepson, four year old Daniel Pelka in July 2013, and he is now serving life, with a minimum tariff of thirty years. Labour MP Geoffrey Robinson demanded to know why Krezolek was not deported, even though he had been arrested at least six times for a number of different offences. The answer is quite simple, Poland and the UK are members of the EU and because of this, if anyone wants to come to this country from Poland they can, even if we kick them out they can then return and there is very little we can do about it. If we want to control our borders, and who comes into this country, we need to gain independence and then we can control who comes into the UK.

Second. All permanent settlement needs to be halted NOW!—that also includes allowing asylum seekers into the country. We cannot afford to allow the amount of people to come into this country, for the reasons I have outlined above.

Third. We need to break the benefits culture. Currently there are about 8 million people in this country not working, about 2.5 million officially unemployed and about 5.5 million on some sort of incapacity benefit. This needs to change, I believe that many of those on incapacity benefit could probably work, but do not want to, or have been told by a doctor that they are suffering from an illness and can't work. Don't misunderstand me, I know there are people who are genuinely ill and disabled and cannot work, I am not talking about them, just those who could work but won't. There are many unemployed who have never worked and have no intention of working. They wouldn't work even if you gave them a well paid job, with good holiday entitlement, and other benefits; such people probably would not bother getting out of bed in the morning. I believe we need to be tough on these people, no more excuses. If someone is given a job and they do not take it, and haven't got a good reason not to take it, there needs to be an impact upon them personally, they need to realise that they do have a choice. As I have written above, we in this country know that if we do not work we will not starve or go without, the state will always provide, and I believe this is one of the problems.

When the welfare state was set up after World War Two, it was set up as a safety net for those that got into trouble. It was probably one of the greatest things any government has ever set up; free health care, child benefits, unemployment benefits. Who could really complain? If you got into a muddle, the state would help. But what we have now is no longer a safety net to catch those who have got into trouble, but a safety blanket. This means that you no longer have to do anything because the state will always provide regardless of whether you have ever contributed or made any effort to help yourself. And this is were the problem arises, many people realise that they do not need to work, so quite simply don't! Surely a better system would be, if you did not work and had no genuine reason for not working you have a gradual reduction in benefits to the point were you would have no choice but to work? The situation that we have at the moment just cannot continue, and if something radical is not done things are not going to change.

Lord Beveridge, whose blueprint for the welfare state was published in 1942, said it should not 'stifle incentive, opportunity or responsibility.' And this is one of the problems we have in this country, that people do not feel that they have to take responsibility. The government has become the parent, and so it does not matter if you work, the government will always be there and will always provide, so why should they work? When Gordon Brown decided to increase welfare to lift people out of poverty, he should have read William Gladstone, who said 'that giving the poor money just keeps them poor'. This is not true for everyone who lives in poverty (the word 'poverty' in this case is relative when compared to many of those in Third World countries, where poverty is absolute. We, I believe in our modern day Britain have not known real poverty, and maybe this is the problem! If people experienced real hunger and deprivation and knew that the government was not going to provide, they might actually want to work). Gladstone's comments, however, have been shown to be true, as many who have been given much in the way of benefits have decided not to work, and have not even looked for work.

There are many who would love a job, but can't get one simply because there either isn't any or they are too low paid, or an employer would rather employ a migrant. We need to make work pay; I understand that if you are getting more on benefits than you could get if you were working, then there is no incentive to work? This is were the benefits system needs to change. At the moment, if you get a job, but were on benefits, you lose a large percentage of your benefits, which might mean you are either worse off or just a few pounds better off. What, then, is the point of working a forty hour week when you would be no better off financially than if you did not work at all? We need a graduated system in which you do not lose all your benefits or most of them when you get a job, and as your money increases with pay rises your benefits are decreased. Also, on this point, we need to increase the tax threshold; the government needs to make it worth while working, and part of this could mean that if you earn under £15,000 per annum you do not pay any income tax. This could be paid for by the reduction in benefits which would naturally come from getting people back to work.

Fourth. I believe immigration needs to be reversed. I believe this can be done, and needs to be done. If it isn't, we are never going to get our unemployed into or back to work. I have outlined above why this is not going to happen; simply by the fact of continuing immigration there is no need for an employer to take on a British worker. Also, because we are part of the EU, we cannot 'discriminate' in favour of a British worker; all 'EU citizens' have the same rights as British workers.

A good example of the idiocy of EU law, is the case of medical staff that come to the UK from within the EU. Under EU law, the Nursing and Midwifery Council is banned form testing nurse's competence and skills and their ability to understand and speak basic English. The tests are deemed to restrict the 'free movement of Labour'—even though the same rules apply to doctors. This policy is incredibly dangerous.

This rule is very likely to lead to someone being given the wrong drugs or not being treated correctly, simply because the nurse or doctor cannot speak English or is not competent enough to be performing their duties. This has actually happened. A German Doctor, Dr Daniel Ubani, was working for an out-of-hours medical service in Cambridgeshire when he mistakenly gave 70-year-old renal patient David Gray ten times the safe dosage of diamorphine. He has since been struck off by the General Medical Council, but because he is a German citizen he is still able to continue to practice in Germany. Fortunately, the government has seen some sense, and, from 1 April 2013, medical staff from within the EU will be tested to prove that they have the 'necessary level of English' to work in hospitals and GP surgeries. The fact that it has taken so long to change this idiotic and very dangerous rule shows how those who are in charge either do not understand or care about those they are supposed to serve!

Fifth. Currently the majority of migrants working in this country are doing unskilled work that British people could easily do. If we are to get people back into employment (and there are many who would love to work), there needs to be the work for them to do. At the moment our economy is barely growing, but jobs are being created, even though the majority are being taken by migrants. The situation with our economy is not likely to change in the near future, so I believe something radical needs to be done.

The vast majority of those who have come to this country are not asylum seekers, neither have they left their country because there are no jobs available. The majority who have come to this country in the past few years have come here to make a better life for themselves and their families, and as I have said before, who can blame them?

This situation might be beneficial for migrants and employers; when talking about immigration and people's concerns politicians continually state that it is good for our economy, and it is what business wants. Politicians from the three main parliamentary parties continue to repeat this mantra, but, hopefully, having read what I have written, you will realise that business will always say this. I hope you realise by what I have written that this issue is a lot more complicated than this simplistic and rather selfish point of view that business and politicians keep repeating.

Unlimited, uncontrolled, unrestricted, permanent mass immigration cannot continue, it is unsustainable; we live in a small country with limited space, limited jobs, limited housing, limited beds in our hospitals, limited school places, etc, which is why something radical needs to be done. And this is what I propose:

All foreign passport holders need to be registered; we need to know who is in this country. Many people in this country are living here illegally and we need to find out who should be and who shouldn't be here. When we have discovered who is living here illegally, we then need to deport them back to their country of origin. Again, I am not talking about genuine asylum seekers, but if a person is here illegally, it either means they have come into the country on a temporary visa and have overstayed their visa, or have somehow managed get into this country by illegal means. So, they should not be here, and need to be removed. There should not be an amnesty, as it has been shown not to work, and more illegal immigrants will continue to arrive.

Nick Clegg claimed in April 2010 that his amnesty for those illegals who had been here ten years would be a "one off" measure. Here are some simple questions for Mr Clegg and his Liberal colleagues;

—What about the following year, when those who have been here nine years would qualify . . . . and so on? To "deal with" the present crop of illegals, the amnesty would have to last for ten years; otherwise it would only deal with a relatively small proportion of the one million or more now here.

—What about proving ten years residence when, by definition, there are no documents?

—What about the risk of fraud? An American amnesty in the mid 1980s was found to attract 75% fraudulent applications from Mexicans.

—What about European experience with amnesties? Here is the experience of Spain and Italy:

Italy

1987/88	1990	1996	1998	2002
119,000	235,000	259,000	308,000	700,000

Spain

1985/86	1991	1996	2000	2001	2005
44,000	135,000	21,000	127,000	314,000	700,000

MigrationWatchUK

In these charts, we can clearly see that even though Italy and Spain have had amnesties, it has not worked and year on year illegal migrants continue to arrive. They are not forced to leave, they remain, the question has to be asked, if amnesties do not work, why do they continue with them? It has quite clearly been shown that amnesties do not work, so that is why we need to remove all illegal immigrants.

Once all foreign passport holders have been registered, we then need to look at the case for them staying in the country. I believe these should be the categories for allowing people to stay in the country:

1. Marriage to a British citizen (with strict criteria to stop bogus marriages).
2. Having a skill and job or money that we need to improve our economy.
3. Genuine asylum seekers.

All foreigners who have committed crimes and have finished their sentence be given no right of appeal. They would be forced to leave the country with no chance to return.

That is it! We should still issue temporary workers visas, but once they have expired, they have to leave. Once this criterion has been set in place we then need to get people back to work. As I have said, there are jobs being created, and the majority of jobs are going to migrants. First, all jobs have to go to British workers, unless they are highly skilled jobs that we need a foreigner to do. But because most jobs being created are jobs that require very little skill, I cannot see that we will need to import labour.

Also, we need to start replacing foreign workers with British workers, and how I propose to do it is to look at what jobs migrants are doing; if we have the skills in the country to do that job, a British worker has to replace that foreign worker. This will mean that the migrant will have to leave his or her job, and a British worker will be trained up in their place. I have written above how I propose to get British workers back to work; and working with the employer, I propose that the foreign worker can stay in the job for a certain amount of time, say six months and then they will have to leave. Their job will be taken by a British worker and the migrant will have to leave the country. If they need financial help in returning to their country, our government can provide it.

You might argue that this is unworkable and unaffordable, because the British worker will have to be paid whilst the foreign worker is being paid as well. What I propose is that the government will pay the wages of the British worker until they are trained, and then once the foreign worker leaves the funding stops. This, I believe, would work because those who are unemployed are getting benefits anyway so it would not cost a huge amount more, eventually we would see the benefits of this policy.

Financially, it would bring massive benefits, as currently there are about 8 million people in this country not working and the majority would go back to work and start paying their way financially. They would not be receiving so many benefits, so would not cost the tax payer so much money, plus they would be earning, and buying goods, thus contributing towards the economy. Add to this, all 'EU citizens' are entitled to receive benefits; we would then make a saving by not paying out billions in benefits to hundreds of thousands of foreigners. This will then free up jobs, houses, school places and a reduction in spending on the NHS and other public services. The money that is in short supply will not have to go so far and will benefit those who should be here.

(Just two points about benefits and 'EU citizens' being able to claim within a very short amount of time of arriving in the UK. Firstly, it could be argued that those who come to this country come here to work, so should be entitled to at least some sort of benefits. I cannot see that this is really fair, simply because entitlement to social security is a privilege of nationality, and the ability to determine who can and can't claim is central to the sovereignty of a state. There is also a basic principle at stake, namely that you shouldn't be able to draw out of a pot that others have filled, but you have not. This, I do not think is at all unreasonable. Secondly, you could say that because migrants who come to this country end up in work, they should be entitled to something from the system, but because the vast majority of migrants who come to this country end up in low paid jobs, they quite clearly pay very little in tax, if anything at all. Thus, because many of those who come here bring family members, the amount they get is far greater than what they pay in, in terms of schooling, the NHS and council services).

Some might say this is extreme, but I do not believe it is; until we do something radical things are not going to change. Unemployment is not falling, even when many private sector jobs are being created. Even taking into consideration job loses in the public sector surely the unemployment figure should have fallen! Immigration into this country has surely had an impact in terms of the unemployment figures.

Houses are in short supply, and I do not believe concreting over many thousands of square miles of beautiful countryside is the answer, as this is one resource that is needed. Not just for growing crops, but also once it is gone it is gone and future generations will not benefit from green wide open spaces. I think we have a duty to our children and grandchildren to look after this wonderful resource.

Once we have immigration under control we can then look at how we handle future migration into this country. Countries like New Zealand, Australia and Canada, etc, have very strict criteria for migrants staying. Canada only allows about 200,000 people to stay in their country every year, and they have to bring benefits to the country, not take from it. If you look at Canada and its size in comparison to ours, it makes you realise how absolutely unsustainable and ridiculous the situation in this country is.

I believe we should be able to decide who we want to come into this country, rather than being forced by an outside authority to allow many hundreds of thousands of people that we cannot afford to live here.

In 2007, Romania and Bulgaria joined the European Union, and countries like the United Kingdom put 'transitional arrangements' in place. In short, whilst the two countries may have joined the European Union, some countries, including the UK, put in a restriction effectively blocking the migration of Romanians and Bulgarians. This changes on the 1 January 2014; as you can imagine, this is going to have an impact upon this already crowded country. The concern is that when the restrictions on these two countries are lifted we will have a similar situation which we had in 2004. The government are stating that it will not be the same because in 2004 it was only a handful of countries which opened their borders. They argue that because all EU countries will open their borders, the people from Romania and Bulgaria who decide to leave will be spread out equally amongst all member countries.

This in itself is rather idiotic, as, why should we have to take any? Simply because they are members of the EU, does it make economic sense, or is it practical? The government does not know how many will come, or, if they do, they will not tell us. Having seen what happened in 2004, when we were told that 13,000 would arrive, you can be pretty much assured that the government does not really know. The simple fact is, as I have already pointed out, there is nothing this government can do to stop this happening, which shows quite clearly that we are no longer an independent country. Whatever your viewpoint on immigration, surely it cannot seriously be argued that this sort of immigration is sensible?

SUMMARY

When I decided to put my thoughts down on paper in regards to the subject of immigration I wanted to try and explain why I feel so strongly about this issue. I hope that I have set out clearly my reasons and why I struggle with the policy of uncontrolled, unrestricted, open door, mass immigration that has been forced upon the people of this country.

Hopefully you have realised in what I have written that I am not against immigration, nor am I against genuine asylum seekers. I have, over a number of years watched as the country I love change, and I do not feel it is for the better.

I have stated my reasons for feeling like this, and I hope you can see where I am coming from. This country has always accepted migrants with open arms; I believe Great Britain is a very tolerant nation; this, I believe, is not a new phenomenon. Many people have come to this country and worked hard and have given this country much. Isambard Kingdom Brunel was the son of a French migrant; you don't have to spend too much time looking to see what an amazing man he was, and the contribution he brought to this country.

Likewise, I am sure if you walk through any town or city in Great Britain, you will find there are many thousands of businesses which were started up by migrants. If you were to contact every migrant in the country, you will probably find the vast majority of them are hard working and have a job. It would be difficult to dispute any of this, but, as you may have realised, that is not the reason why I wrote about this issue.

I have no personal animosity towards any group or people. I do not believe British people are better or better educated (this is clearly not the case, as I am sure many employers will testify). I do not believe migrants are doing anything wrong or illegal; the vast majority are coming here for a better life, and who can blame them? I do not believe that the vast majority of migrants are taking advantage of our generous welfare system; I am sure there are some, but when you look at how many British people who are not working because they do not want to, it isn't any wonder that employers would rather employ a foreign worker.

In saying all I have said, I wanted to explore the reasons why I am against mass, uncontrolled immigration, and I wanted to look at what should be done to halt it, and reverse it. I am not looking to be controversial, but I truly believe if something is not done about the situation in our country, the consequences for the future are very serious.

Many would say that we have always had immigration into this country, and they would be right; that cannot be disputed. We have had mass immigration into this country before; during the fifties and sixties, we had a massive influx of foreigners from The West Indies, Africa and the Indian Subcontinent. Some might argue that this did no harm to our nation; it has been shown that unemployment has gone up and down, and on the whole we have been okay. But what we have now is different.

Basically, we have no control over who comes to this country from the EU, and it is also the sheer scale of immigration. We are living at a time when the old world order is changing; we live in a truly globalized economy. For years, Westernised economies have had it good; Europe, the US and Japan have been the driving force behind the global economy, but all this has now changed. China, India, Brazil, Russia, South Korea, etc, are still seeing growth, even in the midst of a global recession. Great Britain and Europe are seeing very little growth and are cutting jobs. Many countries within Europe are doing the same, and with the Euro in crises it is unlikely to change dramatically in the foreseeable future.

What I want to emphasize, is that I have no problem with people coming to this country to work on a temporary basis. My concern is with those who come here on a permanent basis, as they stay and then use the services which I have listed. This then means they start to take more than they bring.

If you then add into this mix joblessness, and not just this, but no hope of getting a job, with prices rising in everything from food to energy, the pressure on people is going to increase. And, eventually, this could boil over into anger and violence. You might think that sounds dramatic, but I believe we have been very much cocooned in this country and have never witnessed any real deprivation.

We have a fantastic welfare state, free medical treatment, free education; if you lose your house you will not go homeless, and many do not pay towards anything and just live on benefits. How many of us in this country have to beg to live? How many of us have ever gone hungry? How many of us have ever worried about the government's inability to run the country? You might say they haven't done a very good job recently, and I will agree. I know many governments have made mistakes, but we have always had a stable government, and on the whole things tick along okay.

But, I believe that if something isn't done about the very important issue of 'permanent settlement', all we have known and loved could change, and not for the better.

I titled this paper 'immigration—a study in arrogance and ignorance' for a reason. One of the things I have noticed over the years about the political class (i.e. 'the chattering classes', middle class liberals, including many of those who appear on programmes like Question Time), is an incredible arrogance and ignorance. Many believe that their opinion is the only opinion that counts and anyone who disagrees with it is at the very least simply misguided or at the very worse, extreme and most definitely wrong.

I have stated why I believe the policy of mass uncontrolled immigration is wrong, a view shared by many millions of ordinary British people. The vast majority of these ordinary British people are not extremists, they just want to be listened to, and would ask that something is done about this very damaging policy.

It is interesting and upsetting that almost anyone over the past few years who has raised their concerns about the issue of uncontrolled immigration has been accused of being a racist. I do not understand the correlation between the accusation and the reality; to define someone as being racist just because they raise their concerns about uncontrolled open door mass immigration is an extreme reaction. To call someone a racist just because they ask for control over who comes into this country is illogical and would mean that whole countries must be, by this very definition, racist. Are Australia, Canada, New Zealand, Switzerland (who on June 9 2013 voted to tighten the asylum rules by 78.4%) **(20)** run by a bunch of right-wing extremists bent on persecuting foreigners? Are they lacking in compassion? Are they hateful people who detest migrants and want to destroy their lives? Of course not! These, and many countries throughout the world, have sensible immigration policies because they know it makes perfect sense. They know they need to put the interests of their own citizens first, and if they let immigration run out of control it can bring many, many problems. This is in no way unreasonable and should not be seen as such.

When speaking to people about this issue, I have hardly ever spoken to anyone who truly believes that immigration does not need to be controlled. I know that the view I hold and those that I have spoken to are not isolated and in the minority. Every poll that has been taken over the past three years lists uncontrolled immigration as one of the main concerns for British people. In the run up to the 2010 general election, 65 year old Rochdale grandmother, Gillian Duffy, was labelled a 'bigoted woman' by the then Prime Minister, Gordon Brown. His reason for doing so was because she raised her concerns about the amount of Eastern European immigrants living in the UK. Speaking about her two grandchildren, aged 10 and 12, she said she was "concerned about how they would be able to afford to go to university when they are older" **(21)**. This is an example of how those who hold the reins of power are completely out of touch with the ordinary man and woman. Gillian Duffy was not an extremist who belonged to a far right wing party, by her own admission she was a life long Labour supporter. During this same general election campaign the issue of immigration never once dropped out of the top three concerns in all polls **(22)**.

This issue has been consistently ignored; for whatever reason, those in charge, our politicians and bureaucrats, seem to believe this issue should never really be discussed. And I believe that many who hold the reins of power truly believe that they are the ones who should be listened to, and their views count more than the views of ordinary British people. This issue has been consistently ignored, for whatever reason by those in charge, our politicians and bureaucrats seem to believe immigration and the concerns and pressures that people feel should never really be discussed. I believe that many who hold the reigns of power truly believe that they are the ones who should be listened to, and their views count more than the views of ordinary British people. According to Andrew Neather, a former adviser to Tony Blair, Jack Straw and David Blunkett—"relaxation of controls was a deliberate plan to open up the UK to mass migration".

He said "I remember coming away from some discussions with the clear sense that the policy was intended—even if this wasn't its main purpose—'to rub the Right's nose in diversity' and render their arguments out of date". This shows the complete contempt those who are in charge actually feel for those they are supposed to serve!

I have watched, and listened, to politicians and 'the chattering classes' discuss many issues; they espouse a totally politically correct view of the world that most people do not live in. Most of these people live in nice areas of Britain that are not blighted by the problems in our society, they live in a bubble and only occasionally venture out and look at the issue as if travelling to a zoo to watch the animals.

Many politicians have never known any real hardships, they attended public school or were given the chance to attend a grammar school. You only have to look at the front bench of all our political parties to see that the majority of them come from wealth. I know that is not true for all our politicians, but just look at the background of so many and you will see this to be true.

A recent survey of all MPs by the Smith Institute found that 34 per cent went to private schools (and 20 to just one school, Eton), compared with just 7 per cent of the population as a whole. 22 per cent of our MPs have worked in the media, as lecturers or teachers, yet only 4 per cent had manual jobs and less than 2 per cent worked in agriculture. I do not believe this makes you a bad politician, but I do believe this can lead to an imbalance within our political parties and this has been shown to be true by many of the policies and decisions that are made. Many do not understand the reality for so many ordinary people, simply because they have never sat where they sit, have never worked in a 'normal' job, have never felt the pressure of living on an inner city housing estate, and the issues that can come with that.

I have written about what I believe is a massive issue for this nation; I have written what I believe needs to be done about it. This policy was forced on the British people with no consultation, because those in charge believe they are right. This issue, as well as the issue of the EU, is continually ignored, because our politicians believe they know best. If you spend any time looking at the history of government in this country and the world, you will see that those in charge have made many mistakes and driven forward policies which have in the short term and long term brought many problems.

Many politicians have pushed forward policies that are complete folly and fundamentally wrong, misguided and ill thought out. We elect these people in the hope that they know best and they will do a good job, and we hope that they will represent our views, but as we know, on the whole this is not true. Destroying our grammar school system, privatising the railways, selling 400 metric tonnes of gold at its lowest price for 20 years, taking away the dividend tax relief from private pensions, going to war in Iraq, signing up to the Lisbon Treaty and not giving the British people a promised referendum on this treaty. These decisions were made by those in charge, and I don't look back with the benefit of hindsight and state that they were bad decisions; many agreed that they were bad at the time. But the politicians went ahead regardless with their decisions, and this shows incredible arrogance. These are a few quick examples from off the top of my head; if I spent a few hours I am sure I could think of dozens. Add to this list, uncontrolled, open door, mass immigration and you will see that just because those in charge think that something is a good idea does not necessarily mean it is.

In the run up to the 1997 general election, no party stated in its manifesto, a pledge to increase immigration. I do not remember anyone walking around saying "Hey, you know what would be good? An extra few million people in this already crowded country". This quite clearly is not what people would have wanted, and I know this is not what people want. In 1997, immigration wasn't an issue which reared its head in any poll taken, why is it such an important issue now? Is it because the British people have suddenly become racist and now hate all foreigners? Obviously not! Regardless of how many times we are told that immigration is beneficial for this country, does not necessarily mean it is. The simple truth is, this country is very, very crowded and immigration needs to be controlled. Those in power need to listen, because those who elect them are saying enough is enough. But unfortunately they do not care and are not listening, and even if they wanted to do something they cannot, because of our continued membership of the European Union.

I hope that what I have written will make people think. In all that I have written, I wanted to emphasize that my issue is not with the migrant who comes to this country. As I have already stated the vast majority have come to this country to make a better life for themselves. The target for my views are those in power who have forced this policy on us with no concern for the consequences. I believe at the very least there has to be control; regardless of whether you think what I have written here is extreme surely it is only reasonable to do something.

Times change, and I am sure some of the statistics I have used will be out of date by the time you read this, but the issue, nonetheless, has not changed.

I could fill many more pages about immigration and its problems, but I have got to stop somewhere. I just wanted to finish with these quotes. They were taken from an article on the BBC news website about the Welsh county of Gwent in 2013:

There have been many grand schemes for the county and millions have been spent on new roads and other infrastructure projects. But the one vital ingredient, the single commodity the people need more than anything else, has failed to materialise. Work.

"The jobs simply aren't here," says a man nursing a pint in an almost deserted working men's club. "But try telling that to the people at the top and they just don't want to know," he concludes bitterly.

A quarter of working-age adults are on benefits—male unemployment is more than double the British average. Among the economically inactive, the students and the homemakers and the sick, a far higher proportion in Blaenau Gwent say they would like employment than across the country as a whole. These communities are desperate for work.

Official figures show that last year more than 8,000 people wanted a job. But there were just 300 vacancies. And most of those were low wage temporary positions." **(23)**

That sums up the reality, I don't think I need to say anything else.

Evan Heasley
July 2013

SOURCES

This is not a conclusive list of sources, there are many more. I thought I would list the most prominent.

1. http://www.telegraph.co.uk/news/politics/8451986/It-is-Cable-not-Cameron-who-is-stoking-extremism.html

1a. http://www.bbc.co.uk/news/uk-23475230

2. http://news.bbc.co.uk/1/hi/uk_politics/5273356.stm

3. http://www.bbc.co.uk/news/uk-20681551

4. http://www.telegraph.co.uk/news/uknews/6395813/Britains-population-to-hit-70-million-by-2029.html

5. http://www.bbc.co.uk/news/uk-14663354

6. http://www.appgmigration.org.uk/sites/
   default/files/APPG_migration-twelve_
   months_governemnt-briefing.pdf

7. http://www.taxpayersalliance.com/
   highspeedrail.pdf

8. http://www.bbc.co.uk/news/
   business-16467903

9. http://www.warmwell.com/windfarms.html

10. http://www.telegraph.co.uk/news/politics/
    liberaldemocrats/8074669/Danny-Alexander-
    reveals-500000-job-cuts-in-document-gaffe.
    html

11. http://www.bbc.co.uk/news/10604117

12. http://www.bbc.co.uk/news/10604117

13. http://www.ons.gov.uk/ons/rel/lms/
    labour-market-statistics/december-2012/
    statistical-bulletin.html

14. http://www.dailymail.co.uk/news/election/
    article-1264333/GENERAL-ELECTION-
    2010-Under-Labour-nearly-UK-jobs-taken-
    foreigners.html

15. http://www.telegraph.co.uk/news/
    uknews/1895759/Crimes-committed-by-
    European-migrants-up-by-800-per-cent.html

16. http://www.itv.com/news/
london/2012-04-05/atm-crime-spike-feared/

17. http://www.appgmigration.org.uk/sites/
default/files/APPG_migration-twelve_
months_governemnt-briefing.pdf

18. http://www.bbc.co.uk/news/uk-england-
south-yorkshire-22604081

19. http://www.bbc.co.uk/news/
business-21522522

20. http://www.swissinfo.ch/eng/swiss_news/
Minister_pushes_for_more_asylum_reforms.
html?link=tdj&cid=36094414

21. http://news.bbc.co.uk/1/hi/8649476.stm

22. http://migrationobservatory.ox.ac.uk/
briefings/uk-public-opinion-toward-
immigration-overall-attitudes-and-level-
concern

23. http://www.bbc.co.uk/news/
magazine-23028078